I0795074

To Leonardo and Jade, our companions in adventure

Blue and wild

Amazing marine animals of **Baja California**

Cecilia Soldatini
Yuri V. Albores Barajas

Illustrations by
Monica Parussolo

SUNSET & VENICE

IUCN

The International Union for Conservation (IUCN) of Nature's Red List of Threatened Species is the world's most comprehensive information source on the global conservation status of animal, fungi, and plant species.
You can scan this QR code or type www.iucnredlist.org and search for the scientific name (you'll find it in the ID card of each species), so you can explore information about distribution, see photos, and much more.
Have fun!

A Peninsula and its Menagerie

Horacio de la Cueva

In the imaginary world of European explorers, Baja California was an island. Today, we know it is actually a peninsula—almost an island—filled with landscapes, mythical characters, and fascinating secrets. The peninsula resembles and arm jutting out from California, surrounded by two very vivid and contrasting seas. The west coast of the peninsula faces the Pacific Ocean, which brings cold waters from the north and tropical waters from the south. Its eastern coast embraces the Gulf of California, also called the Sea of Cortez. The oceanographic conditions in both seas bring about high productivity, making life within rich and diverse. Jacques Cousteau called the Gulf of California, "the world's aquarium."

Our imagination has known and created fantastic animals based on descriptions, interpretations, fantasies, dreams, fears, and nightmares, all inspired by reality. The bestiaries, ancient books that illustrated these animals, can never surpass the biological reality and richness that evolution has blindly created. We are surrounded by animals, plants, and microscopic life that defy our imagination in their true form, where and how they live.

The book you hold is not an encyclopedia of the sea animals of the peninsula. It is as fantastic a narration as any bestiary, but it is founded on the natural and scientific knowledge we have of each species. Each animal shown here has a valuable life which we have the privilege and responsbility to love, care for, and keep alive and thriving.

Pelicans are quite peculiar birds, possessing a **very long bill** with a **large gular sac**. When you see an adult pelican feeding a chick, you may be surprised to see the chick poking its head inside the gular sac, searching for regurgitated food. The chick searches rather aggressively, and although the pouch may appear so fragile that the chick's bill will pierce the skin, in fact, the sac is perfectly built for this.

You can see the brown pelican **flying very close to the sea's surface**, almost touching it with the tips of their wings and exercising very little effort, instead using the air pressure between their wings and the water.

Then, they do something very unusual for a seabird: they cross the land on the US-Mexico border, heading for the ocean and reaching not only the Channel Islands but also the busy piers of San Francisco. When crossing land and heading to the Pacific Ocean, they can most likely no longer see the sea—quite an adventure for a seabird. This **long journey**, from the tropical paradise of the La Paz and Los Cabos coasts to the colder and richer waters of San Francisco, is not without danger for the young, as well as the more experienced birds.

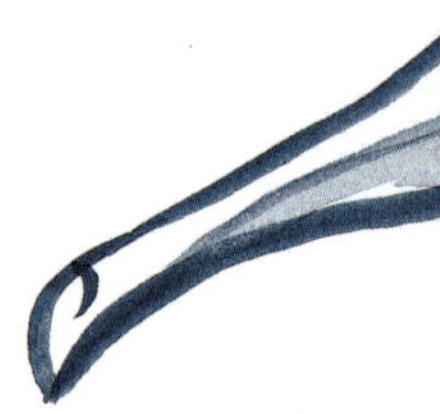

01 Brown Pelican

From the Malecon in La Paz to the Piers in San Francisco, Always in the Coolest Location

ID Card

- **Scientific name:** *Pelecanus occidentalis*
- **Wingspan:** 6.5 feet (2 m)
- **Weight:** 11 pounds (5 kg)
- **Lifespan:** About 30 years
- **Diet:** Fish, especially sardines
- **Reproduction:** Lays 1 to 3 eggs in a nest made of sticks on the soil or cliffs; breeding is asynchronous, from December to June
- **Conservation status:** Least concern
- **Peculiarities:** They usually dive from heights of 100 feet (30 m) in an arrow shape, using their weight to reach high speeds and dive deeper into the water

In fact, the giant **nets** used in sardine fisheries in the Gulf of California pose a serious danger to pelicans, as they often get trapped when trying to steal sardines and may suffer life-threatening injuries or even drown. It is also not easy for young birds to learn how to dive and fish, and they can injure their wings or neck while practicing.

As with many species of seabirds, the competition for food is high, and humans are the main competitors, catching large quantities of **sardines**, the pelican's favorite food!

The pouch of the pelican is made of skin, which also covers the entire bill, except for the hooked tip. They use this pouch as a net to catch fish, drain the water, and then swallow their prey directly from the pouch; they don't need teeth or a sharp bill to eat.

The largest fish in the world feeds on the smallest organisms in the ocean? Although it seems weird, it's true. The whale shark is a **filter feeder** and feeds on tiny **plankton**. Whale sharks can reach 60 feet (18 meters) long, while plankton are less than a millimeter in size, which is why whale sharks feed in areas where there are plenty of plankton to be found.

Whale sharks like **warm tropical waters**, such as those found in the Gulf of California. There are two sites in particular where it is easy to spot and swim with these giant fish: Bahia de los Angeles and Bahia de La Paz. It is a unique and unforgettable experience if one is lucky enough to set eyes on these creatures. The whale sharks salute you from afar, raising the tip of their tail fin out of the water.

When they get closer, you can see something star-like moving underwater: these are the **white**

02 Whale Shark

The Gentle Giant

spots on the fish's back. These spots are unique to each whale shark, and you can identify whether you are swimming with one individual or another, as each animal can be identified by the pattern of their white spots.

There is little information about these gentle giants, but there are many people trying to learn the most important aspects for their conservation, including what troubles they face at sea, where their offspring are born, what areas they visit on their travels, etc.

Whale sharks swim about **15 miles** (25 kilometers) **per day** and can make some tremendous long-distance oceanic journeys. For instance, scientists recently tracked a female whale shark from the eastern Pacific to the western Indo-Pacific for 12,515 miles (20,142 kilometers) over 841 days—the longest Whale shark migration route ever recorded!

ID Card

- **Scientific name:** *Rhincodon typus*
- **Size:** 60 feet (18 m)
- **Weight:** 9.8 tons (9 metric tons)
- **Lifespan:** 50 to 100 years
- **Diet:** Plankton, small squid, krill, and small fish
- **Reproduction:** Offspring develop inside of an egg the mother's body. They are not born all at once, but rather in a prolonged period. The mom gives birth to live young 16 to 24 inches (40 to 60 cm) long
- **Conservation status:** Endangered
- **Peculiarities:** Spotted back

Whale sharks filter and strain plankton, small squid, krill, and small fish with their gills for nourishment. They also have 3,000 tiny teeth around 1 inch (2.5 centimeters) long, but they don't use them to eat.

03 Laysan Albatross

The Luminescent Cyclist

ID Card

- **Scientific name:** *Phoebastria immutabilis*
- **Wingspan:** 83 inches (210 cm); it is one of the smallest albatrosses
- **Weight:** 8 pounds (3.5 kg)
- **Lifespan:** The albatross is 70 years old and is the oldest known living wild bird
- **Diet:** Mainly squid
- **Reproduction:** They lay one single egg, weighing 25 percent of the female's weight
- **Conservation status:** Near threatened
- **Peculiarities:** Large black eyes

Albatrosses are the **largest birds on Earth**—they can reach 11.5 feet (3.5 meters) from end to end of their wings! On land, albatrosses are clumsy. They have an awkward waddle and their landing form is reminiscent of a potato sack.

The Laysan albatross is among the smallest of its family, however, in comparison to other birds, it is still very large. It is one of the **four species** of albatross living in the northern hemisphere and breeding on the Pacific islands. One of those islands is the Mexican island of **Guadalupe**, which is 161 miles (260 kilometers) from the Baja California Peninsula.

When albatrosses land, they perform a special **dance** with their partner to show how happy they are after a foraging trip at sea. Facing each other, they execute a very coordinated sequence of movements with increasing speed. This is their courtship. The courtship is a dance with a very clear message: "If you are not capable of dancing with me, how can we be partners?" For this reason, they put a lot of effort into such dances. At the same time, they emit **vocalizations** similar to whistles. The dance ends with their heads straight toward the sky.

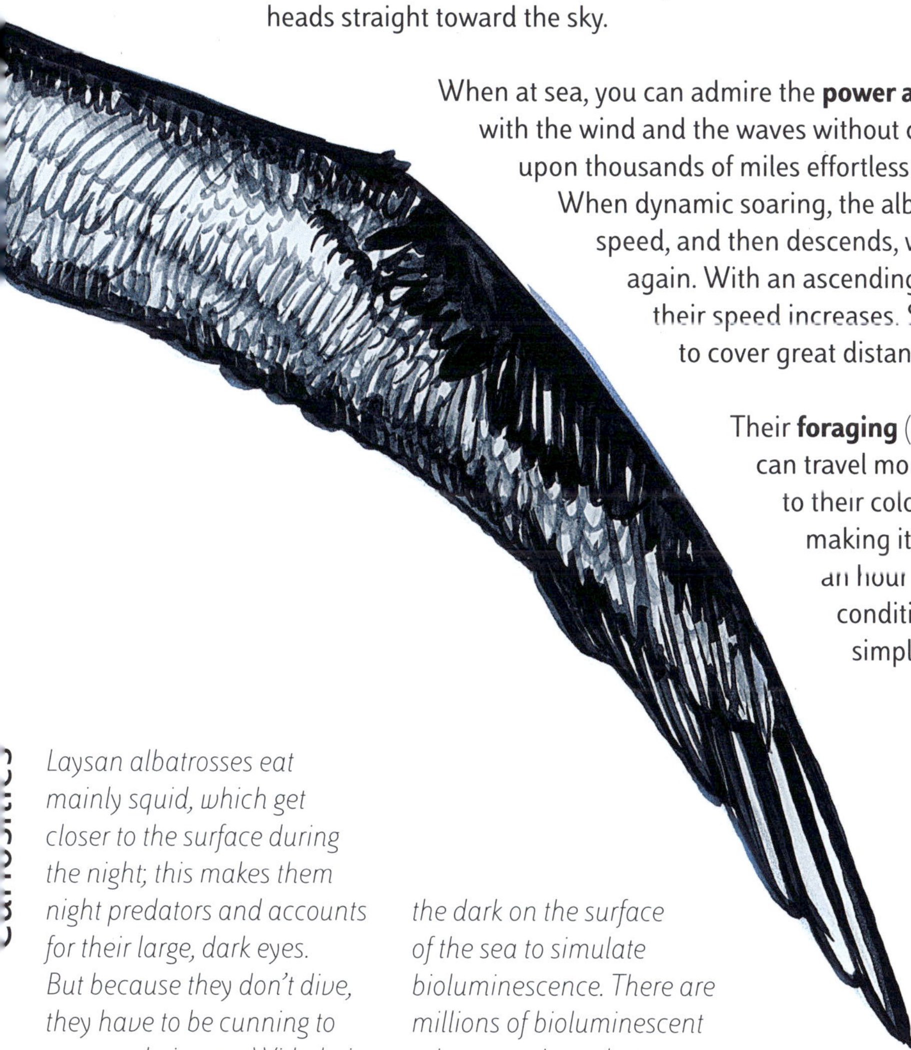

When at sea, you can admire the **power and agility** of the albatross, watching as they soar with the wind and the waves without closing their wings. They can travel thousands upon thousands of miles effortlessly, circumnavigating the globe in some cases. When dynamic soaring, the albatross increases its height and decreases its speed, and then descends, where it can increase speed before ascending again. With an ascending force created by the pressure under the wing, their speed increases. Such force allows albatrosses and other seabirds to cover great distances without flapping, just gliding.

Their **foraging** (feeding) **trips** can last 15 to 18 days, and they can travel more than 5,000 miles (8,000 km) before returning to their colony. Strong wind increases their flying speed, making it an ally to them. They can reach up to 62 miles an hour (100 kilometers an hour) with good wind conditions. When the wind is weak, however, they simply float on the water.

Laysan albatrosses eat mainly squid, which get closer to the surface during the night; this makes them night predators and accounts for their large, dark eyes. But because they don't dive, they have to be cunning to capture their prey: With their powerful sense of smell, they distinguish the areas with the highest concentration of organic carbon (which indicates the presence of squid). They then pedal in the dark on the surface of the sea to simulate bioluminescence. There are millions of bioluminescent microorganisms that create sparks when the water is disturbed, so squid come close to the surface. If there is light, they are attracted to it. Simple, incredible, and magical!

04 Vaquita

The Panda of the Sea

ID Card

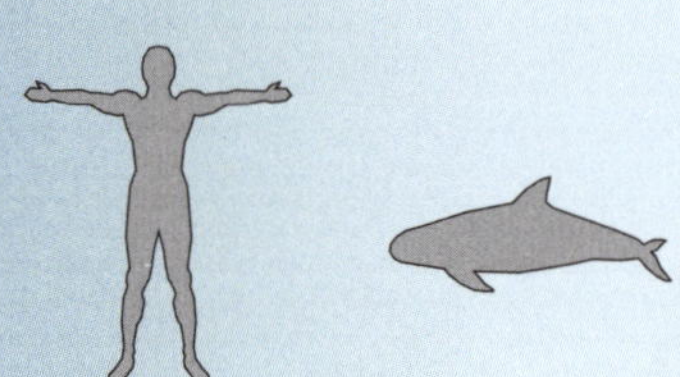

- **Scientific name:** *Phocoena sinus*
- **Size:** 5 feet (1.5 m)
- **Weight:** 121 pounds (55 kg)
- **Lifespan:** Up to 20 years
- **Diet:** Squid and benthic fish species
- **Reproduction:** Can breed every other year
- **Conservation status:** Critically endangered
- **Peculiarities:** It is the smallest porpoise of the world

On the **northern part of the Gulf of California**, there is a marine mammal that can be found here and nowhere else! Its name is vaquita, though it is not a relative of vacas (Spanish for cows) that decided to go back to the sea. Rather it is an **odontocete cetacean**, like dolphins and orcas; more precisely, it is a **porpoise**. It has a short snout and rounded head.

The vaquita is the only porpoise species that lives in **warm waters**. All its close relatives live in temperate waters, under 68°F (20°C). This is because the vaquita is a relict species that historically had a much wider distribution. They arrived in a glaciation and could not escape due to subsequent heating, so they remained confined to the northern part of the Gulf of California. Although temperatures decreased, the species remained there, adapting to the local conditions.

The area inhabited by the vaquita consists of shallow and cloudy waters, and therefore the species needs to use **echolocation**, like a bat, to find food. This same area is home to the totoaba, a fish species of high commercial value, but its fishing is illegal, as it is a protected species. To capture the totoaba, fishermen use nets that also capture vaquitas, drowning them and bringing the population to the **brink of extinction**.

Vaquitas, like other porpoises, are normally seen alone or in small groups of two to three individuals. They begin reproducing at three years old and can only breed every other year, making the species **slow to recover**.

In 1997, 597 individual vaquitas were estimated to be living. IN 2019, only 17 were remaining. We can only hope this species still survives as you read this book.

Curiosities

The vaquita has dark circles around the eyes—because of this, they are also called the panda of the sea. They are the smallest cetaceans of the world. Little is known about their ancestors' biology, as they were discovered less than 60 years ago, and we are close to losing them forever.

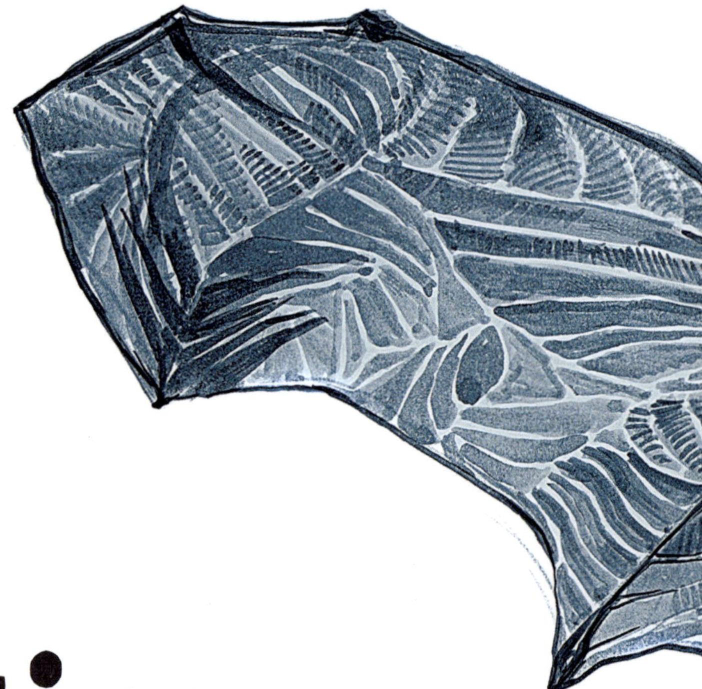

05 Fish-Eating Bat

The Night Fisher

ID Card

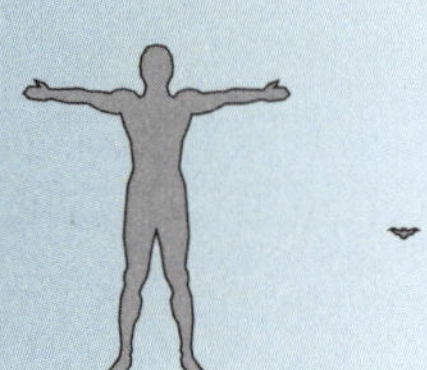

- **Scientific name:** *Myotis vivesi*
- **Size:** 5.4 to 6.4 inches (138 to 163 mm)
- **Weight:** 0.9 oz (27 gr)
- **Lifespan:** Up to 30 years
- **Diet:** Fish and crustaceans, occasionally small insects
- **Reproduction:** Give birth to young in spring
- **Conservation status:** Vulnerable
- **Peculiarities:** The tail is long and extends beyond the edge of the uropatagium. Its legs are inverted and hydrodynamic to be able to hunt without affecting its flight

Bats eat fish too! There are several species of fish-eating bats, but the fish-eating myotis, *Myotis vivesi*, is the only bat that **fishes in the sea** despite the waves and the wind.

Inhabiting **narrow cracks** and **hollows** in the rocks and cliffs near the sea, it is found only on the islands and coasts of northwestern Mexico (the peninsula of Baja California and Sonora). The bat comes out when the diurnal birds are no longer heard and the stars begin to shine. Until sunlight reaches the surface of the sea, the bats hunt for **small fish and crustaceans**, sometimes flying in circles before the catch.

The fish-eating bat is considered a **rare species**, but **locally it is common**. The largest colony has been estimated between 12,000 and 15,000 individuals on Isla Partida. Due to the introduction of **predators**, such as mice and cats, on the islands where it lives, the Myotis is considered endangered.

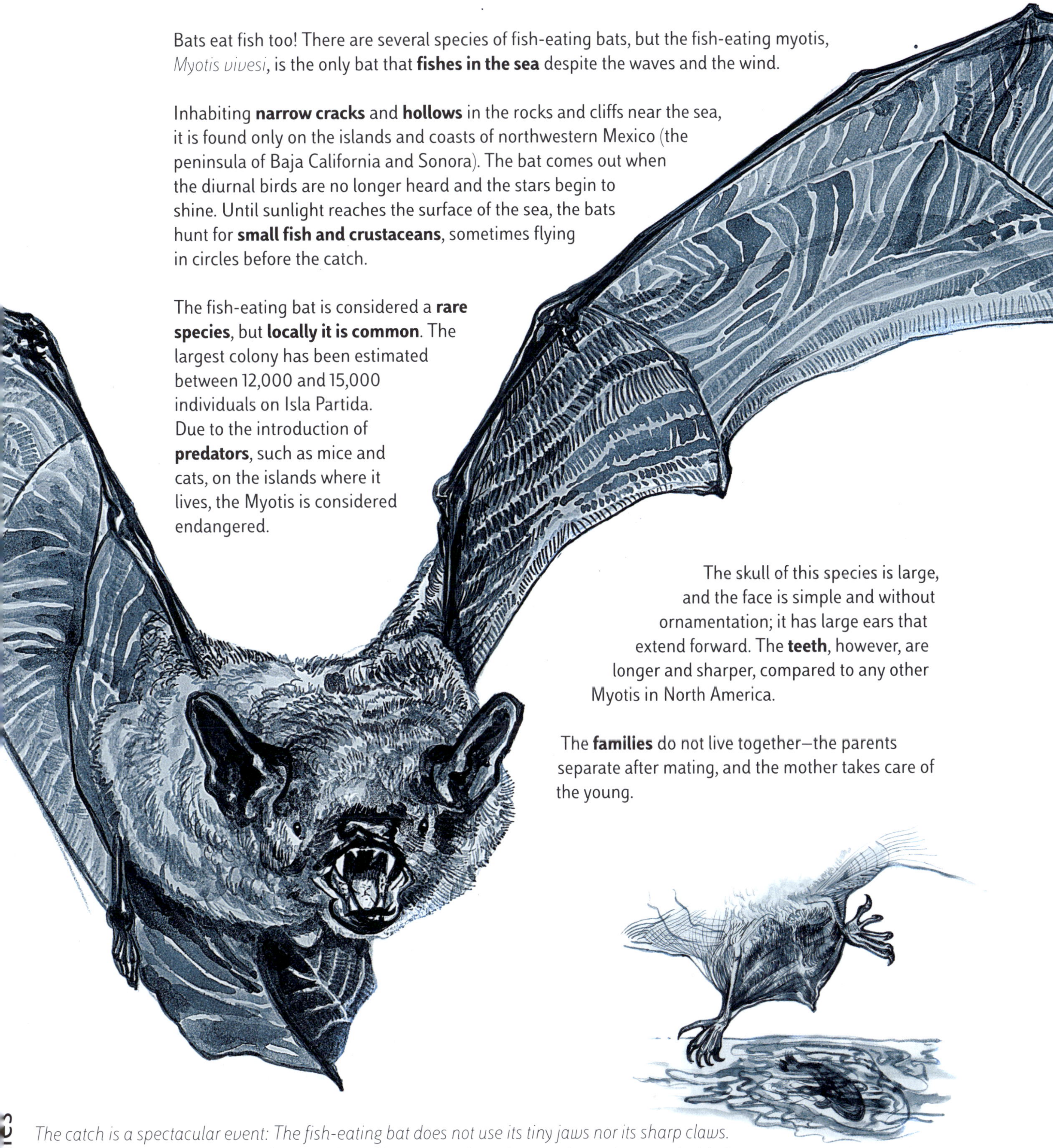

The skull of this species is large, and the face is simple and without ornamentation; it has large ears that extend forward. The **teeth**, however, are longer and sharper, compared to any other Myotis in North America.

The **families** do not live together—the parents separate after mating, and the mother takes care of the young.

The catch is a spectacular event: The fish-eating bat does not use its tiny jaws nor its sharp claws. Instead, it catches its prey using the extension of its uropatagium, the membrane between its hind legs and tail. Without falling into the water, they manage to take a spoonful of seawater in which their prey was swimming and then immobilize it with their claws to transport it to their refuge. All of this happens in total darkness using echolocation!

The sailfish, one of the fastest and fiercest predators of the tropical seas, lives in the deep blue waters of the Pacific Ocean off the peninsula of Baja California. It gets its name from a highly developed **dorsal fin** that allows extreme **agility and speed**, which are both greater than that of the white shark–one of its top predators. This means that it is on the highest tier of the food chain.

The sailfish sails the oceans, almost always alone, looking for schools of fish. Once it finds a group, it surrounds them and begins a frantic underwater dance. It is a **silver swordsman** with its elegant deep-sea color cape.

At the beginning of **its hunt it changes color**, turning brown to confuse the prey. Once the sailfish reaches the prey, they are stunned with a blow of its sword-shaped beak. The school vanishes, and the sailfish swallows its prey. After so much excitement, it observes the empty blue all around: it'll have to start looking again.

Finding sailfish is not easy–you must **follow the frigatebirds** (see page 25) to find marine predators that hunt the fish near the surface. Seeing the frigates feed at the edge of the water, we can infer that there is possibly a sailfish in action. This is how fishermen find them. If the seamen stayed to watch the dance of this spectacular swordsman underwater, they would not fish it.

06 Sailfish

The Fastest in the West

ID Card

- **Scientific name:** *Istiophorus platypterus*
- **Size:** 10 feet (3 m)
- **Weight:** Up to 220 pounds (100 kg)
- **Lifespan:** Up to 12 years
- **Diet:** Pelagic school fish
- **Reproduction:** The female releases her eggs into the water column while the male releases his sperm; the reproductive period peaks from August to October
- **Conservation status:** Least concern
- **Peculiarities:** Females are generally larger than males

Unfortunately, it is one of the most in-demand **sport-fishing** prizes.
In fact, the most dangerous predators for sailfish are humans. They look for them as trophies because of the difficulty in catching them, but the individuals caught are always smaller: 90 to 110 pounds compared to 990 pounds a few years ago.
This indicates that the population has been, and is being, affected.

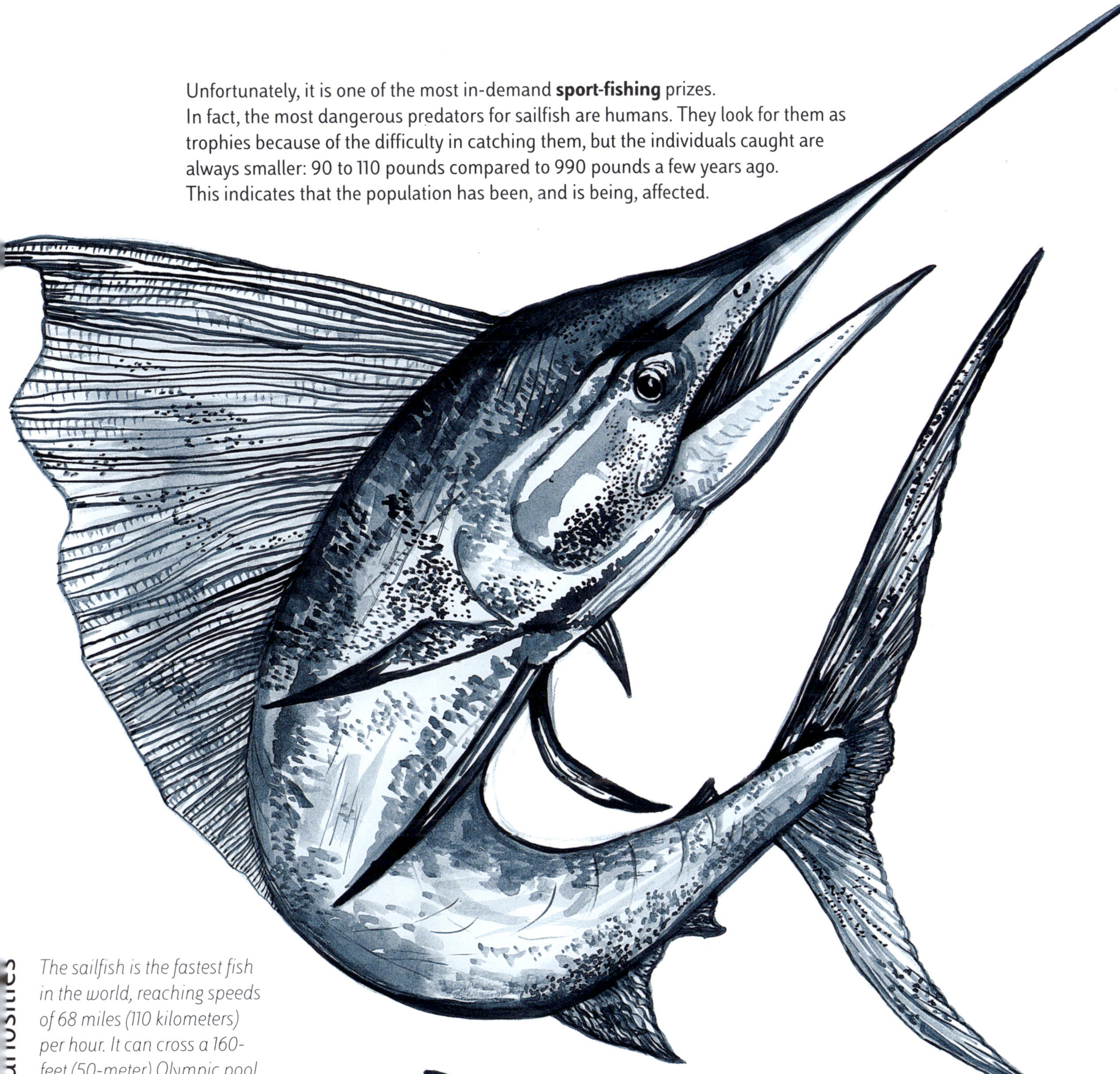

The sailfish is the fastest fish in the world, reaching speeds of 68 miles (110 kilometers) per hour. It can cross a 160-feet (50-meter) Olympic pool in less than two seconds—an Olympic swimmer takes 21 seconds.

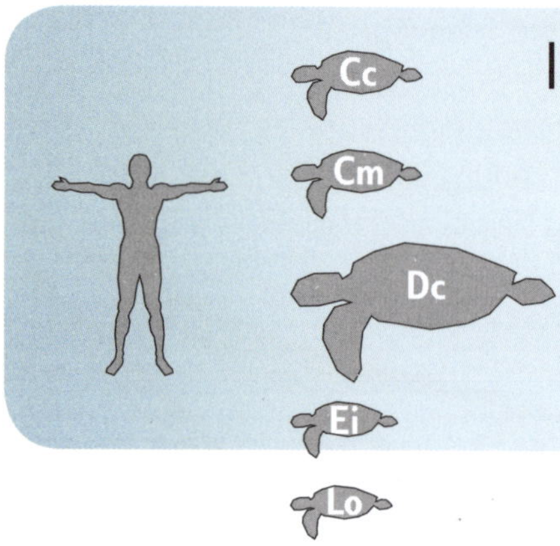

ID Card

- **Scientific name:** Loggerhead *Caretta caretta* (**Cc**), Green turtle *Chelonia mydas agassizi* (**Cm**), Leatherback *Dermochelys coriacea* (**Dc**), Hawksbill *Eretmochelys imbricata* (**Ei**), Olive ridley *Lepidochelys olivacea* (**Lo**)
- **Size: Cc**: 31 to 43 feet (80 to 110 cm); **Cm**: 32 to 45 feet (83 to 114 cm); **Dc**: 59 to 90 feet (150 to 230 cm); **Ei**: 28 to 37 feet (71 to 95 cm); **Lo**: 25 to 34 feet (65 to 86 cm)
- **Weight: Cc**: 154 to 374 pounds (70 to 170 kg); **Cm:** 242 to 419 pounds (110 to 190 kg); **Dc**: up to 2,000 pounds (900 kg); **Ei**: 101 to 154 pounds (46 to 70 kg); **Lo**: 77 to 99 pounds (35 to 45 kg)
- **Lifespan: Cc**: 70 to 80 years; **Cm**: 70 years; **La**: 40 to 50 years; **Ei**: 50 to 60 years; **Lo**: up to 50 years
- **Diet: Cc**: carnivore; **Cm**: herbivorous as an adult;

07 Sea Turtles

The Long Journey of the Sea Turtle

Dc: eats mainly jellyfish; **Ei**: eats anemones, sponges, and crustaceans; **Lo**: omnivorous; eats crustaceans, fish, and algae

- **Reproduction: Cc** y **Cm**: 20 to 25 years old; **Dc**: from 25 to 35 years old; **Ei**: begins to breed when 7 to 13 years old; **Lo**: 10 to 20 years old. They lay between 100 and 150 eggs at a time, depending on the species
- **Conservation status: Cc**: vulnerable, **Cm**: endangered; **Dc**: vulnerable; **Ei**: critically endangered; **Lo**: vulnerable
- **Peculiarities: Cm**: The largest ever recorded was 60 inches (152 cm) and 870 pounds (395 kg)!; **Dc**: The champion of sea turtles: it is largest, dives deepest, and travels the farthest of all sea turtles. The largest ever recorded was 120 inches (305 cm) and 2,019 pounds (916 kg), like a small car! **Lo**: The smallest sea turtle in the area

On a warm autumn night, **baby turtles** (hatchlings) make their way out of the sand of the golden beaches and crawl, with much effort, to the sea, guided by the **reflection of the stars**. That journey across the sand is very dangerous due to seabirds and land predators that could catch them before they reach the waves. When they finally arrive at the water, they begin a journey that will last many years. These little travelers will cross oceans, grow, and eventually find a mate to reproduce with.

On their trip, the turtles take advantage of the protection of **vegetation pools**, where they can also find algae and small prey to feed on. Gradually, their **leather shell** will grow and become **harder**, protecting them from predators so they can leave the shelter of their hiding places. Occasionally, however, sea turtles see little bits of colorful **plastics** and **floating bags**, getting confused and eating the trash instead of their usual meal of crustaceans and jellyfish. Eating this litter can result in a slow and painful death.
If they survive the many dangers of the ocean, such as ghost fishing nets and pollution, sea turtles will mate at sea. Afterward, female turtles will swim to the beach where they were born many years earlier and crawl until they pass the tide line. There they will dig a **deep hole** and lay **hundreds of round eggs**. The **temperature of the sand** will determine whether **males or females** will be born to continue the circle of life.

Of the **seven species** of sea turtles, **five live in the seas of Baja California**. Three species come to Baja California beaches to breed: the olive ridley, which regularly nests in the area, and the leatherback and green turtles, which sometimes nest there.

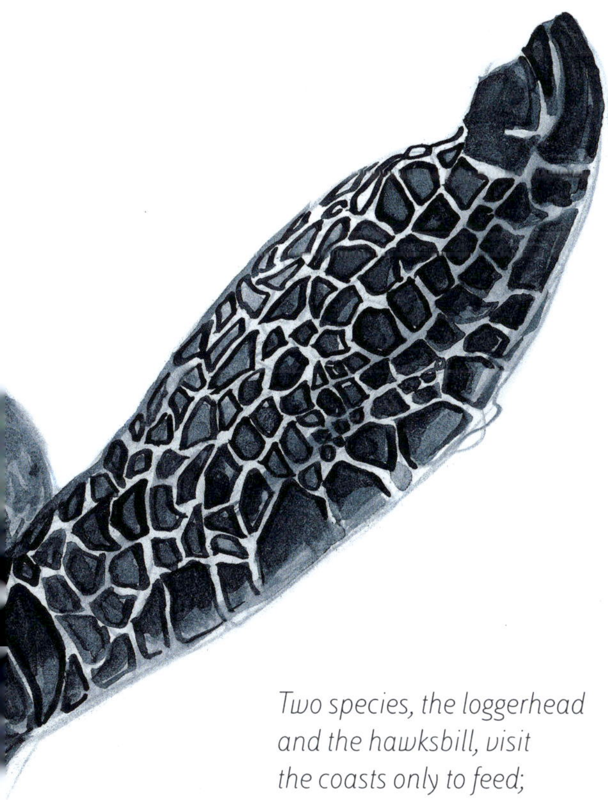

Curiosities

Two species, the loggerhead and the hawksbill, visit the coasts only to feed; the loggerhead breeds in Japan. This means that on their travels they often cross the Pacific Ocean to move between their nesting and feeding areas.

Named the "red devil" by local fishermen in the Gulf of California due to its **intense red color**, the Humboldt squid is definitely interesting. Its **large size** and **ferocity** have only added to its nickname. The Humboldt squid's growth rate is one of the fastest recorded in the animal world. However, such size is not a barrier to the amazing **speed** and **maneuverability** this creature possesses.

The Humboldt squid has **eight muscular arms** and **two tentacles**, each with up to **1,200 suckers**. Each sucker can be lined with up to 24,000 small sharp teeth to catch its prey, making it almost impossible for prey to escape.

The red devils move by **jet propulsion**, making them extremely fast and able to attack in less than a second. They hug their prey with their arms and tentacles, moving them toward a chitin beak capable of ripping pieces off the prey.

Not usually a solitary animal, the Humboldt squid typically attack in groups. There have been observations of clans with up to 1,200 individuals, coordinating an attack on prey much larger than themselves. To distract the prey, the Humboldt squid **changes colors**. When they feel they are at risk of being attacked, they excrete ink to escape from predators.

It is impossible to observe these creatures during the day, as they are several hundred meters below the surface. However, at dusk, they make a **vertical migration** toward the surface, where the low light

08 Humboldt Squid

The "Red Devil"

ID Card

- **Scientific name:** *Dosidicus gigas*
- **Size:** It can reach up to 6.5 feet (2 m)
- **Weight:** Up to 110 pounds (50 kg)
- **Lifespan:** Up to 2 years
- **Diet:** Small fish, crustaceans, cephalopods, and copepods
- **Reproduction:** Females may lay more eggs than any known cephalopod (octopus, squid): up to 20 million eggs! They reproduce via internal fertilization and lay large egg masses of at least 1 million eggs
- **Conservation status:** Data deficient
- **Peculiarities:** Squid have three hearts. The brain/body ratio makes them one of the most intelligent animals

conditions are ideal and plenty of food can be found. Once their prey is caught, they take it to great depths, so that it will pass out due to the lack of oxygen, making it easier to feed on them. In the absence of alternative prey, some squid may exhibit **cannibalistic behaviors**.

The Humboldt squid are attracted to bright lights at night, making it easier for fishermen to catch them. Ultimately, these extraordinary predators deserve our respect and admiration, and our efforts for their conservation.

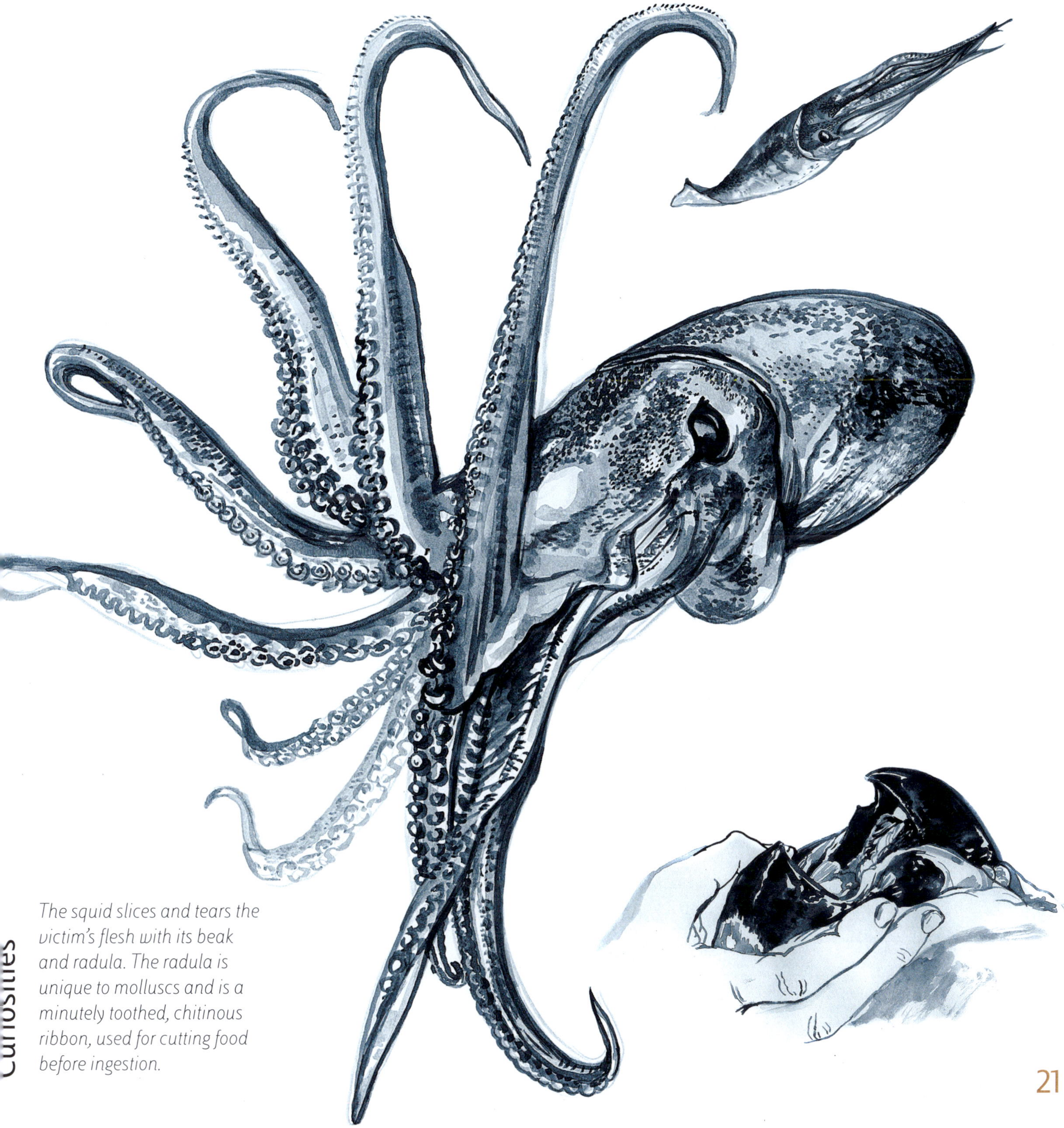

The squid slices and tears the victim's flesh with its beak and radula. The radula is unique to molluscs and is a minutely toothed, chitinous ribbon, used for cutting food before ingestion.

ID Card

- **Scientific name:** *Eschrichtius robustus*
- **Size:** Calves are 15 feet (4.5 m) long at birth; an adult can reach 49 feet (15 m).
- **Weight:** Calves weigh 1,300 lbs (600 kg) at birth; an adult can weigh up to 44 tons (40 metric tons).
- **Lifespan:** Estimated 50 to 60 years
- **Diet:** They feed on invertebrates from the water column
- **Reproduction:** Sexual maturity at 5 to 11 years, or when their size is 36 to 39 feet (11 to 12 m)
- **Conservation status:** Least concern
- **Peculiarities:** The color pattern on the back helps to identify different individuals of the same species

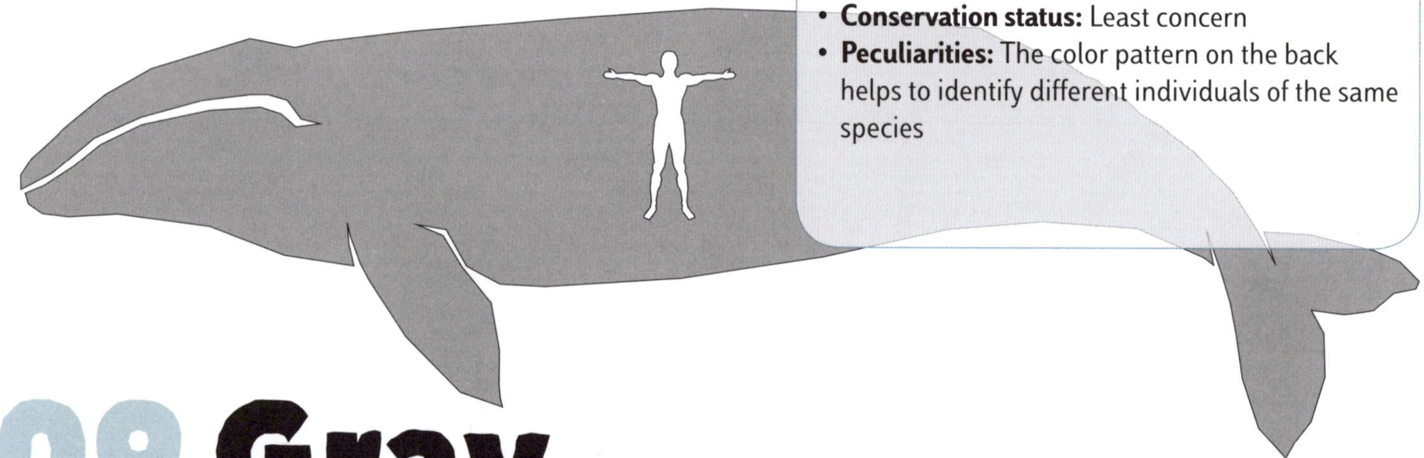

09 Gray Whale

Unbelievable Migrator

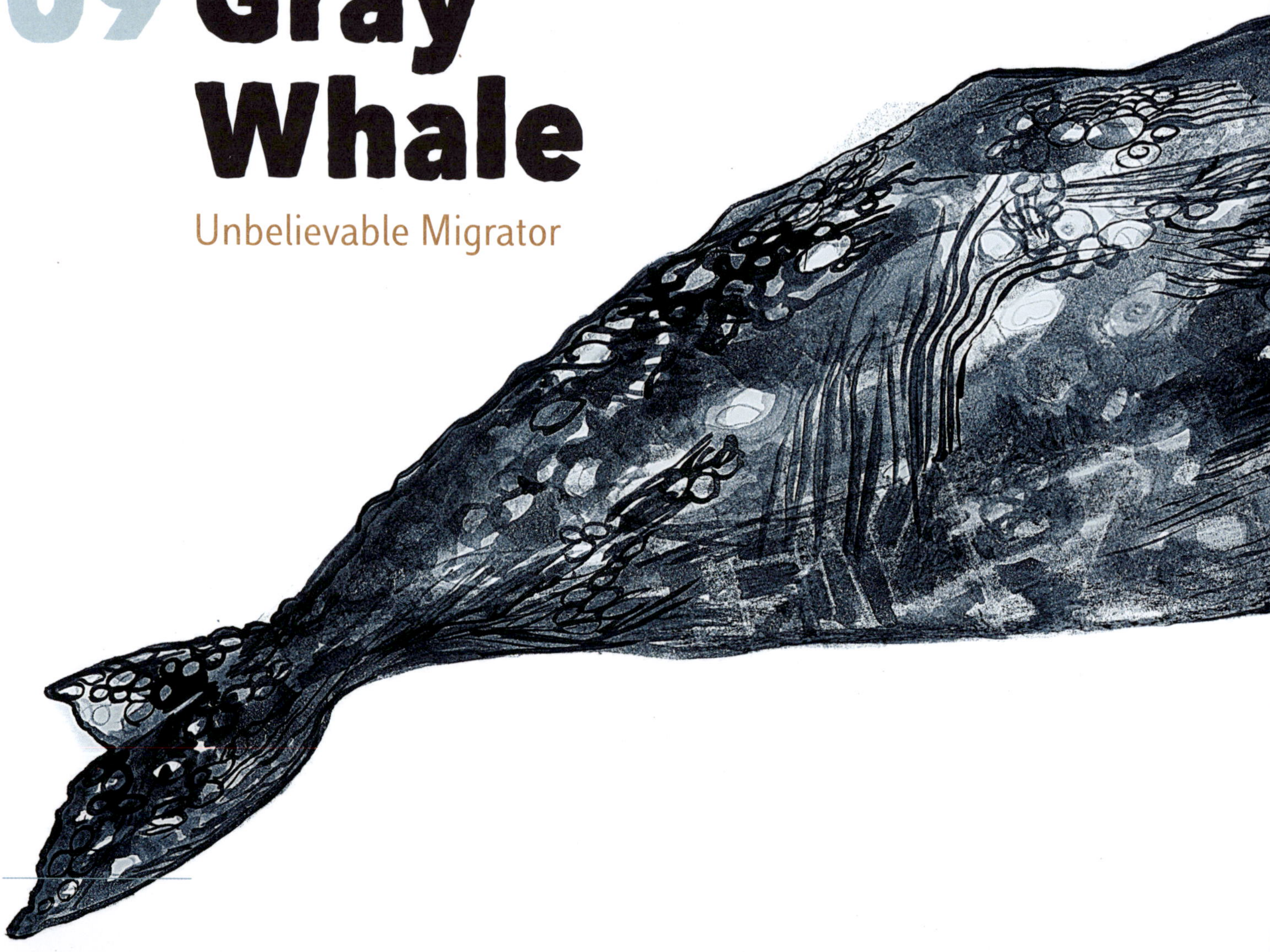

One of the largest **migrations** on Earth actually occurs in the sea, in the Pacific Ocean to be specific. You see, the gray whale makes a round trip of **more than 12,000 miles annually**—from the highly productive waters in Alaska and Canada, where they feed and accumulate reserves, to the coastal lagoons in Baja California, where they mate and give birth to a single calf. The mother whales feed the **calves** for seven months, with a fat-rich milk (53 percent fat, compared to 2 percent in human breast milk). The calves drink 190 liters of milk on average per day.

Adult gray whales have a body covered by **barnacles**, but calves do not have any – they acquire them through their life.

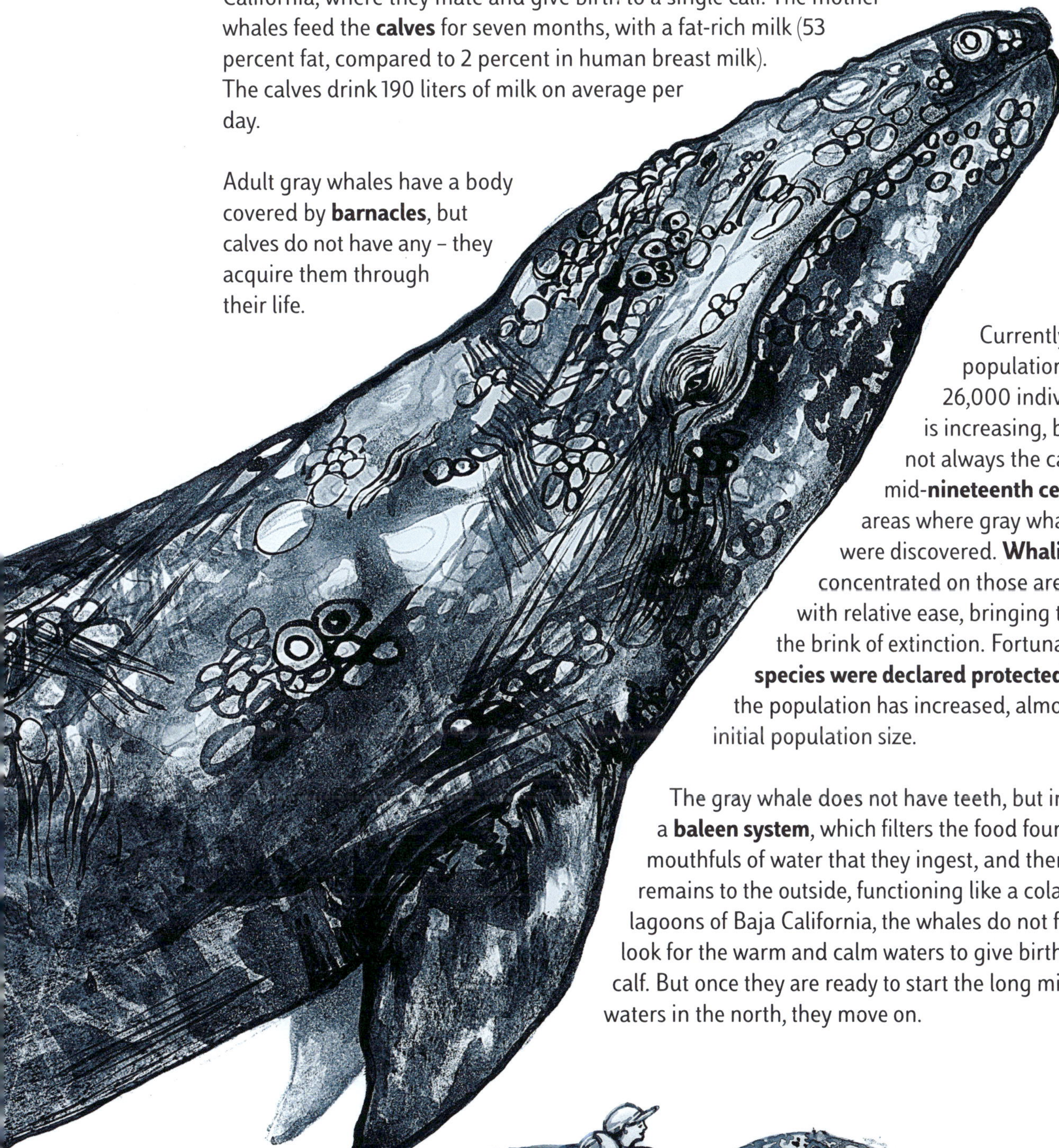

Currently, the world population is around 26,000 individuals and is increasing, but that was not always the case. In the mid-**nineteenth century**, the areas where gray whales gave birth were discovered. **Whaling ships** concentrated on those areas to hunt them with relative ease, bringing the species to the brink of extinction. Fortunately, **in 1947, sea species were declared protected**, and since then, the population has increased, almost reaching the initial population size.

The gray whale does not have teeth, but instead has a **baleen system**, which filters the food found in large mouthfuls of water that they ingest, and then presses remains to the outside, functioning like a colander. But in the lagoons of Baja California, the whales do not feed. There they look for the warm and calm waters to give birth and nurse their calf. But once they are ready to start the long migration to colder waters in the north, they move on.

On the lagoons of Ojo de Liebre, San Ignacio, and Magdalena Bay, it is possible to get close to the whales, and if you are lucky, even touch the friendly whales!

10 Magnificent Frigatebird

The Seabird that Can't Get Wet

A lion allergic to dust? A cold polar bear? Or a seabird that can't get wet? The first two may not exist, but let us introduce to you the third: the frigatebird, a wonderful **seabird that cannot wet its feathers**, although its life depends on the sea. Despite deriving from the same family as pelicans and cormorants, the frigatebirds have **no webbed feet** and **no waterproofed feathers**. These features are what make it impossible for a wet frigatebird to take flight from the water.

When the frigatebird chick is born, it is covered with snow-white down. The parents lay only one egg, taking care of it and defending it against the other males. The danger is not that the other birds prey upon the egg but that they steal the sticks from the nest to build their own instead.

Once hatched and able to fly, one can observe the mother birds who, with lightness and agility, approach as close as possible to the surface of the sea. And upon seeing that a sardine chased by a dolphin is swimming upwards, she will sink her beak and catch it, before quickly regaining altitude. That's it, child's play! The chicks look at them in amazement. They will copy their mother's movements, perhaps trying a few times and learning to follow the routes of dolphins and tuna, who push the prey near the surface where the frigatebird can catch them without risking falling into the water and losing the ability to fly. **Learning to eat and drink without getting wet takes a lot of time**. This makes parental care very long, lasting more than a year. The mother is in charge, while the

ID Card

- **Scientific name:** *Fregata magnificens*
- **Wingspan:** 7.5 feet (2.3 m)
- **Weight:** 3.3 pounds (1.5 kg)
- **Lifespan:** Up to 20 to 30 years
- **Diet:** Their favorite prey are flying fish
- **Reproduction:** Females breed, laying one single egg every two years, while males breed every year
- **Conservation status:** Least concern, although most populations are declining. The largest world colony disappeared from Baja California Sur in the last 15 years
- **Peculiarities:** Their feathers weigh more than their skeleton

father leaves the nest after two to three months. At eight months it is time for the chicks to spread their wings and start practicing. **Speed** and **attention** are needed to be able to return to the nest with a full stomach!

A frigatebird can cross the peninsula of Baja California up to three times a day without effort, in the event it fails to decide where it prefers to eat. If, after eating, they want to rest a little, they can sleep on the wing, especially at sunset, when the sky turns pink and orange. The **foraging trips** can last several days. To rest, the frigates **sleep on the wing**: half of the brain rests while the other half is awake to control their environment. When they return to land, it is important they rest to recover. The frigates are luminous creatures that, without flapping their wings, observe the world in silence.

Females are black with white chests and larger than males. Males are completely black with a red pouch they inflate during courtship.

An underwater airplane? No, it is actually a giant manta ray, one of the largest fish in the world. The giant manta ray is a **relative of sharks**, although with many adaptations they appear less frightening, apart from their size of course. Rather than pointy and sharp teeth, these fish have **several rows of small square teeth**, which are used for reproduction, rather than feeding.

Like the gray whale and whale shark, they feed on plankton, which they need to consume in large quantities to meet their energetic needs. The plankton is so small that it is not necessary to chew.

On the contrary, the giant manta ray can reach up to seven meters. And its intelligence is not far behind. The giant manta has the **largest brain of all fish**. They also have a pair of fins next to the mouth, which helps them channel the food into their mouth. To stay alive, it is necessary for the mantas to be in **constant motion**, so that the oxygen-rich water passes through their gills. And to keep healthy, they visit **"cleaning stations"** so that different species of fish eliminate parasites from their skin.

Giant manta rays were once abundant in the Gulf of California, but **overfishing** led to an absence that spanned several years. Only recently there have been some sightings, so it is necessary to protect them and allow them to return in larger numbers. Despite their size, they are completely harmless to humans, so they depend on our help to survive.

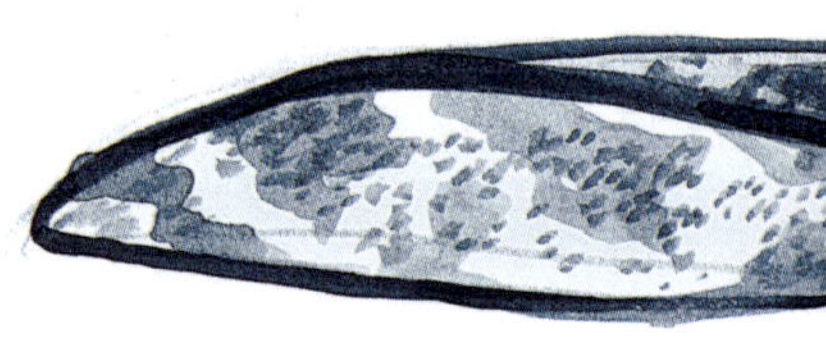

11 Giant Manta Ray

The Majestic Sea Angel

ID Card

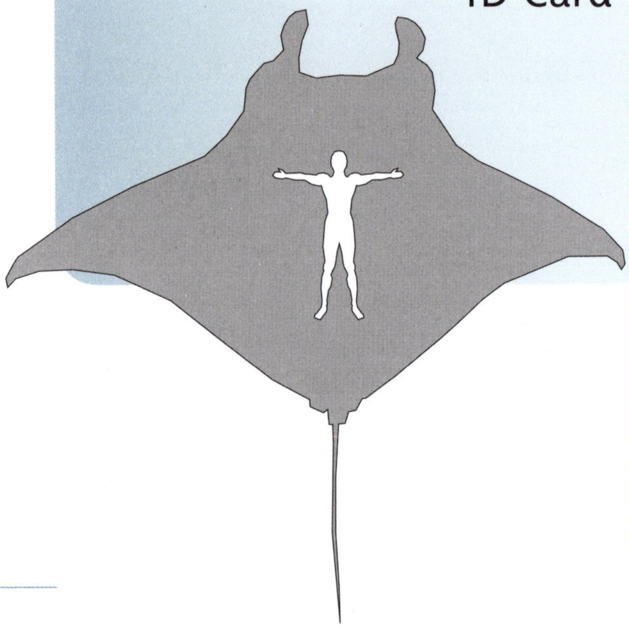

- **Scientific name:** *Mobula birostris*
- **Size:** Up to 23 feet (7 m)
- **Weight:** More than 1.1 ton (1 metric ton)
- **Lifespan:** Up to 50 years
- **Diet:** Plankton
- **Reproduction:** They reach sexual maturity at 10 years and produce a baby every three to four years
- **Conservation status:** Endangered
- **Peculiarities:** Different individuals are identified by colored marks on the body

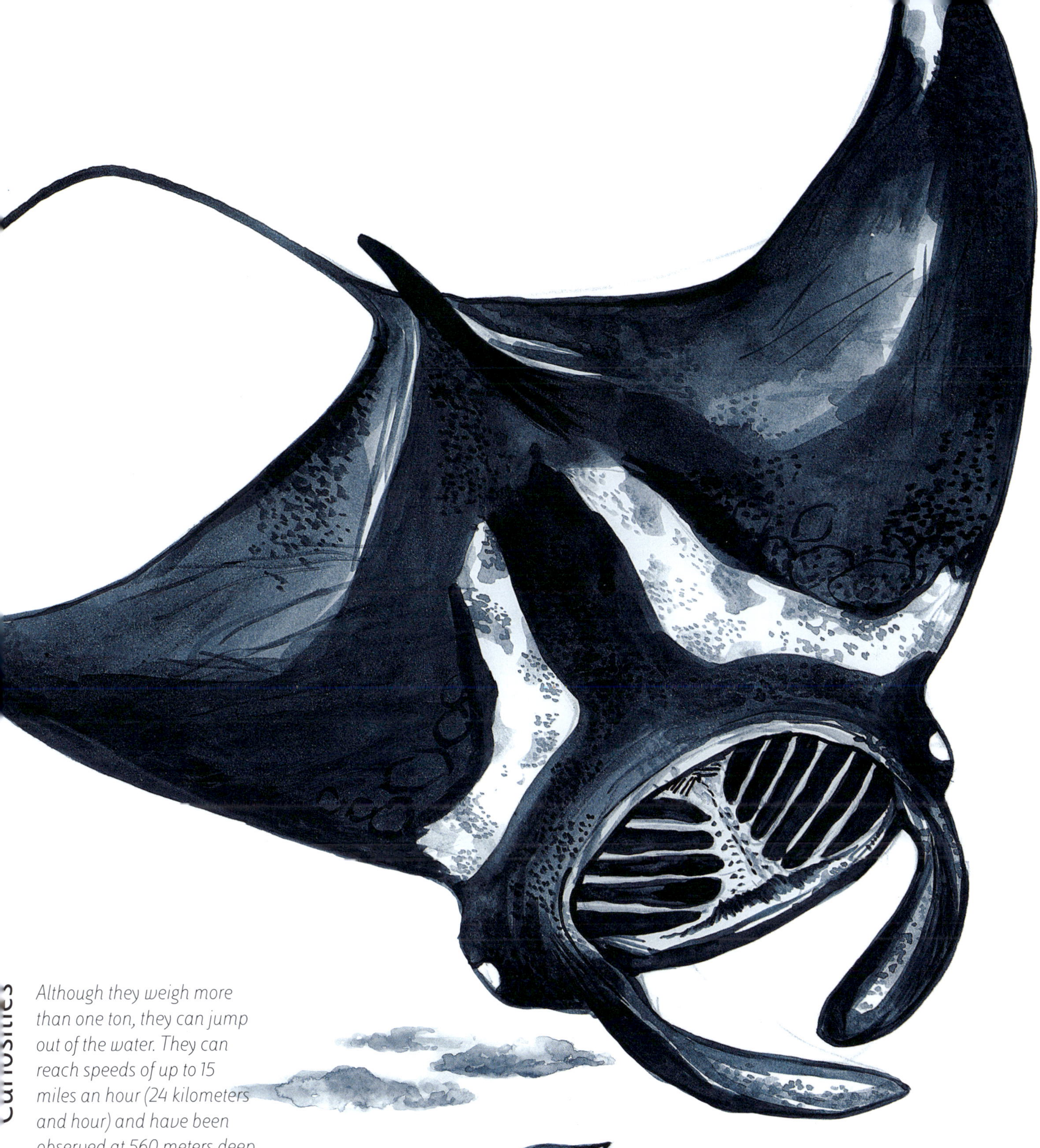

Although they weigh more than one ton, they can jump out of the water. They can reach speeds of up to 15 miles an hour (24 kilometers and hour) and have been observed at 560 meters deep.

There are some **islets**, here and there, in the Gulf of California that simply look like a pile of stones, full of cracks and crevices. These small, dark caves hide fresh air and provide silence when the sun is high and the waves break on the reefs. It is here that storm petrels are **hidden in the day**, unknown to others. Storm petrels are dark colored, nocturnal, and the smallest seabirds in the world. They are companions to the fishermen during **stormy days**—the only conditions in which they will approach the land in daytime. Their kingdom is the night.

In the moonlight, storm petrels disappear **silently** into these cracks and crevices; they appear uninhabited. But when **darkness** falls, thousands of entirely black petrels fly in the night and travel between the sea and their nests to bring to their chicks what they have fished.

Thousands of **black shadows** move like little ghosts against the starry sky—the only noises are those of the sea lions yawning, the waves that caress the stones, and a slight flurry of wings. As soon as the light of the moon or dawn arrives, the magic is interrupted. The sky is left empty, the flurrying of the wings disappears—the petrels are already at sea.

Petrels fish and hunt on the surface of the water, but they are also very good divers. These birds can reach more than **10 meters deep**, and considering their very small size, it is quite the incredible dive!

12 Storm Petrel

Mysterious Inhabitants of the Night

ID Card

- **Scientific name:** Least storm petrel: *Hydrobates microsoma;* black storm petrels: *Hydrobates melania*
- **Wingspan:** 12.5 inches (32 cm) and 20 inches (51 cm), respectively
- **Weight:** Least: 0.6 ounces (18 gr) Black: 2 ounces (58 gr), respectively
- **Lifespan:** Up to 30 years
- **Diet:** Microzooplankton
- **Reproduction:** Lays one single egg weighing 25 percent of the mother
- **Conservation status:** Least concern, although populations are decreasing
- **Peculiarities:** Their bodies are so light that they can fly with a breath of wind

Storm petrels possess no defense against predators: their beak is as soft as rubber and their webbed legs are quite small and fragile, so they are **very vulnerable**. Within the same colony, different species may live together, such as the **least storm petrel** and the **black petrel**, which weighs just 1.5 pounds.

The least storm petrel is the smallest seabird in existence, but it is from the same family as the albatrosses, the world's largest seabirds.

Cecilia Soldatini

Cecilia fell in love with the sea when she was young; sailing and diving have been her favorite sports. After her behavioral ecology and environmental sciences studies between Italy and Scotland, she specialized in studying seabirds. She arrived in one of the seabirds' paradises, the Baja California islands in Northwestern Mexico in 2006. She is the mum of two fantastic kids and enjoys sharing her love for sea creatures with them and every curious young explorer. As a researcher at CICESE, she is involved in several research and conservation projects of marine and island wildlife and ecosystems and teaches graduate and postgraduate students about the animals she loves and hopes to protect.

Yuri V. Albores Barajas

Yuri has traveled the world thanks to the birds. He has studied and specialized in biology in Mexico, England, Scotland, and Italy. His projects and collaborations have taken him from the "roof of the world," in the Sagarmatha (Everest) National Park, to islands in northern Scotland, to islands on the Mediterranean, to the Falklands in the South Atlantic. A few years ago he moved with his family to the Baja California Peninsula, where he currently is a professor at the Universidad Autónoma de Baja California Sur. His passions are seabirds in general, and albatrosses, shearwaters, and storm petrels in particular. He has already had the opportunity of observing many seabird species in person, but the list keeps growing! He currently studies several seabird species in the Gulf of California and in the Pacific.

Monica Parussolo

Monica Parussolo is an illustrator, illustration teacher and creative director of an editorial series. She is devoted to the arts with a special look to nature which deeply inspires and leads her. Her works have been selected for competitions and exhibitions; she is included in the catalogue Annual of the Italian Illustrators 2022.

2022 © SUNSET & VENICE, LLC

Text
Cecilia Soldatini
Yuri V. Albores Barajas

Introduction
Horacio de la Cueva

Illustrations
Monica Parussolo

Translation check
Sara Degonia
Paul Norton

Design and layout
Italo Meneghini

Editorial review
Anna Martinelli
Giovanni Simeone

Prepress
Fabio Mascanzoni

First edition: 2022
ISBN: 978-1-952643-02-6

Published and distributed in the United States by
SUNSET & VENICE, LLC
www.sunsetandvenice.com - contact@sunsetandvenice.com
T. 323 522 4644

Distributed in Mexico by Moscatel BCS s.a. de c.v.
www.bajacaliforniagallery.com - info@bajacaliforniagallery.com

Distributed in Europe by Sime Srl
www.simebooks.com - info@simebooks.com
T.+39 0438 402581

© ALL RIGHTS RESERVED
All images presented in this book are protected by copyright and belong to SUNSET & VENICE. No part of this publication may be reproduced or transmitted in any form, or stored in any retrieval system without written permission of the copyright owner.